Features of Toho Beads

Large Holes - The size of the holes in Toho beads allows for threading multiple strands of thread or thicker thread, increasing the variety of beadwork you can achieve.

Light Weight - The larger hole means less weight so you get more beads when you buy by weight. There are approximately 111,800 size 11/0 Toho beads per kilo.

Toho Triangle Beads

Small & Large Round

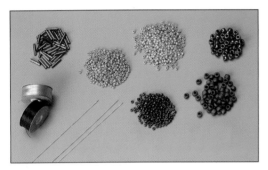

Basic Supplies: Toho Beads • Beading Needles • Beading Thread • Sharp Scissors

How Glass Beads Are Made

Preparation - Silica powder and soda ash are mixed with coloring agents.

Liquefaction - The mixture is melted in a kiln for about 20 hours at 1300°F.

Tube Making - In a kiln, glass is pulled into long thin shapes while air is blown into the center to form long tubes.

Cutting - The tubes are cut to approximate bead size by a blade spinning at extremely high speed.

First Baking - Cut pieces are placed in a 700°F rotating kiln to form round beads.

Cleaning - Beads are washed.

Finishing - Beads are heated in an electric kiln and polished to a high shine. Then various processes - coloring, lustre finishes, metallic finishes - are applied to the beads to enhance their beauty.

Beads to Wear... Every day and Everywhere!

Repeat steps 1 through 7 to make as many panels as needed to complete your bracelet. Cut two 12" pieces of elastic cord and thread through outer rows of each panel to connect them as shown in illustration 8. Or cut 3 pieces of elastic cord and thread them through outer rows and center row of panels. Add beads between panels if desired.

Place cut ends side by side and tie overhand knots to secure. Gently pull to hide any knots inside the beads.

8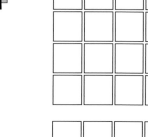

Each of our bracelets was made using a random mix of colorful cube beads, but you can create your own pattern if you like. Copy the blank panels below and color them in with crayon or colored pencils to create your own special panel bracelet.

panel bracelet

Designed by Marilou Porth

1 Thread your needle with 48" of doubled thread. Pick up a bead and pass through it twice in the same direction. Do not split the thread. Leave about a 12" tail. *(Illustration 1)*

2

	1	2	3	4	5	6

Row 1: String on 5 cube beads.
Row 2: String another cube and stitch it to bead #5 as shown in illustration 2.

3

1	2	3	4	7	6

String another bead and stitch it to bead # 4 as shown in illustration 3.

4

1	2	3	8	7	6

5

1	9	8	7	6
10				

You are making thread circles that hold the beads next to each other. Continue in this manner until you have reached the end of the row. *(Illustrations 4 - 5)*

6

11				
10	9	8	7	6
1	2	3	4	5

Row 3:
Add another bead to begin the row as shown in illustration 6.
Continue to add beads across the row.

7

21	22	23	24	25
20	19	18	17	16
11	12	13	14	15
10	9	8	7	6
1	2	3	4	5

Rows 4 & 5:
Work as for Row 3. Remove the stopper bead and weave the ends of the thread through the panel to secure. Your finished panel should look like illustration 7.

Materials:

Gold
6 grams 4mm cube #22
6 grams 4mm cube #22A
6 grams 4mm cube #221
42 gold-filled 2mm
21 gold-filled 5mm
Three 12" pieces of .8mm
    Elasticity

Blue
6 grams 4mm cube #82
6 grams 4mm cube #86
6 grams 4mm cube #566
21 fire polish 4mm
42 size 8/0 #86
Three 12" pieces of .8mm
    Elasticity

Red
4.5 grams 4mm cube #5BF
4.5 grams 4mm cube #25C
4.5 grams 4mm cube #221
1 gram 8/0 #329
21 silver-lined fire polish
    4mm
Two 12" pieces of .8mm
    Elasticity

Basic Supplies:
Size 10 or 12 beading
    needle
Size D beading thread

Pull the thread through slowly and arrange the beads as shown in illustration 3.

Pass the needle through the next bead to the right. *(Illustration 3)*

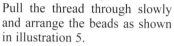

Pull the thread through slowly and arrange the beads as shown in illustration 4.

Pass the needle through the next bead to the right. *(Illustration 4)*

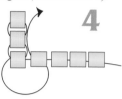

Pull the thread through slowly and arrange the beads as shown in illustration 5.

Pass your needle through the next bead as shown. Pull the thread through slowly. Continue to stitch the remaining beads in this manner. Turn the piece on its side and arrange the beads as shown in illustration 6.

Fold the strip of beads in half as shown in illustration 7. Stitch the first bead to the last bead as shown in illustration 8. Stitch the beads together to hold the rows in place.

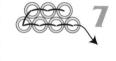

Remove the stopper bead. Tie the ends in a knot and clip the ends of the thread.

Repeat steps 1 through 8 for a total of 9 connectors.

To attach the button to an end connector, thread your needle with 36" of doubled thread. Tie your thread on a connector and weave until your needle comes out of the second bead from the left on the side with four beads. Pick up 5 Treasure beads and pass your needle through the button shank. Pick up 5 more Treasure beads and pass your needle down through the third bead from the left of the connector. *(Illustration 9)*

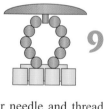

Reinforce the connection by passing through the circle of beads several times. Leave your needle and thread attached and set aside.

To make the beaded loop at the opposite end of the bracelet, thread your needle with 36" of doubled thread. Tie your thread on a connector and weave until your needle comes out of the second bead from the left on the side with four beads.

Pick up 25 Treasure beads and pass your needle down through the third bead from the left of the connector. *(Illustration 10)*

Bring your needle up through the second large

treasure bracelet #2

Designed by Marilou Porth

Purple Bracelet
5 grams 3.3 Treasure #503
1 grams 1.8 Treasure #566
1 grams 1.8 Treasure #711
3 grams 1.8 Treasure #503
3 grams 1.8 Treasure #934

Teal Bracelet
5 grams 3.3 Treasure #601
2.5 grams 1.8 Treasure #7BD
2.5 grams 1.8 Treasure #23
2.5 grams 1.8 Treasure #506

Gold & RedBracelet
5 grams 3.3 Treasure #557
1 grams 1.8 Treasure #22
3 grams 1.8 Treasure #329
3 grams 1.8 Treasure #421

Basic Supplies:
Shank button for clasp
Size 10 or 12 beading needle
Size D beading thread
Scissors

Spacers:

Thread your needle with 36" of doubled thread. Pick up a bead and pass through it twice in the same direction (be careful not to split the thread). Leave about a 12" tail as shown in illustration 1. This is called the stopper bead and it is there to prevent the working beads from coming off the end of the thread. You may have to move the stopper bead down the tail from time to time to make room for the working beads.

Thread on seven 3.3 Treasure beads. Move the beads down to the end of the thread against the stopper bead. Pass your needle back through the next to last bead as shown in illustration 2.

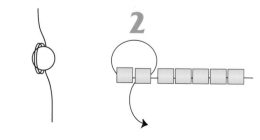

Treasure bead from the left. Pick up a small Treasure bead, skip the first Treasure in the loop and pass your needle through the second Treasure in the loop. Pick up another Treasure. Skip the next bead in the loop and pass your needle through the second bead. *(Illustration 11)*

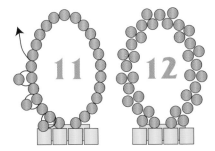

Continue in this manner around loop. Make sure the new beads "share" the space as shown in illustration 12. Reinforce by passing your needle through this circle of beads several times. Leave your needle and thread attached.

Using the needle and thread from the loop connector, thread on beads and connectors according to patterns at right. At the end of a row, pass your needle through the corresponding large bead of the end connector, then bring the needle up through large bead next to it and work back up the bracelet. Use thread from toggle end to work some of the rows as well. Add thread as needed to complete bracelet.

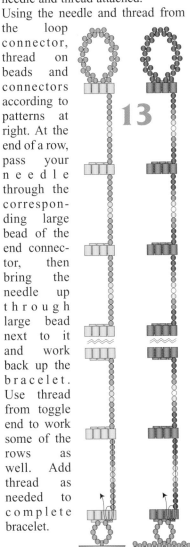

treasure bracelet & necklace #1

Designed by Marilou Porth

Materials:

Purple 18" Necklace
2 grams 3.3 Treasure #503
6.5 grams 1.8 Treasure #503
Approximately 325
   assorted accent beads in
   coordinating colors

Teal Bracelet
2 grams 3.3 Treasure #601
5 grams 1.8 Treasure
   Mix of #23, #506, #566, #711
100-120 assorted accent beads
   in coordinating colors

Fire Bracelet
2 grams 3.3 Treasure #610
5 grams 1.8 Treasure #611
100-120 assorted accent beads
   in coordinating colors

Basic Supplies:
Shank button for necklace clasp
Size 10 or12 beading needle
Size D beading thread
Scissors

Spacers:
Thread your needle with 36" of doubled thread. Pick up a large bead and pass through it twice in the same direction (be careful not to split the thread). Leave about a 12" tail as shown in illustration 1. This is called the stopper bead and it is there to prevent the working beads from coming off the end of the thread. You may have to move the stopper bead down the tail from time to time to make room for the working beads. Thread on seven 3.3 Treasure beads. Move the beads down to the end of the thread against the stopper bead. Pass your needle back through the next to last bead as shown in illustration 2.

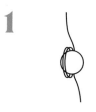

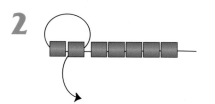

Pull the thread through slowly and arrange the beads as shown in illustration 3. Pass the needle through the next bead to the right. *(Illustration 3)*

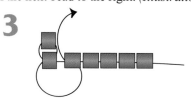

Pull the thread through slowly and arrange the beads as shown in illustration 4. Pass the needle through the next bead to the right. *(Illustration 4)*

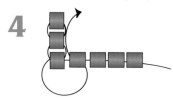

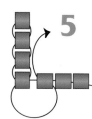

Pull thread through slowly and arrange beads as shown in illustration 5. Pass your needle through the next bead as shown. Pull the thread through slowly. Continue to stitch the remaining beads in this manner.

Turn the piece on its side and arrange the beads as shown in illustration 6.

Fold the strip of beads in half as shown in illustration 7. Stitch the first bead to the last bead as shown in illustration 8. Remove the stopper bead. Tie the ends in a knot and weave them through the connector until they are secure. Clip the ends of the thread. Make 2 connectors.

Toggle: Rows 1 & 2: *For Necklace button clasp, follow the instructions provided in Treasure Bracelet 2 on pages 6 & 7.*
Thread your needle with 24" of thread. String 14

small Treasure beads. Thread on another bead. Skip over one bead and pass your needle through second bead in the row. *(Illustration 9)*

Thread on another bead. Skip over a bead and pass your needle through the next bead in the row. *(Illustration 10)*

Complete the row by stitching the remaining five beads.

Row 3:
Reverse direction. Thread on a bead and pass your needle through the first "tall" bead of the row as shown. *(Illustration 11)*

Add a bead between each of the "tall" beads of the row as shown in illustration 12.

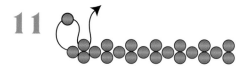

Rows 4 - 8:
Continue to add beads in this manner until you have a total of 8 rows. Peyote stitch is counted on the diagonal. An easier way to count is to add 2 columns. Both methods are shown in illustration 13.

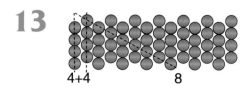

4+4   8

Fold ends together and you'll notice that they fit together like the teeth of a zipper. Stitch the two ends together. Illustration 14 shows you what that looks like if the piece were flat. Weave the ends of your thread through the beaded piece until they are secure. Clip ends close.

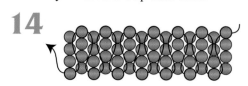

Continued on page 10

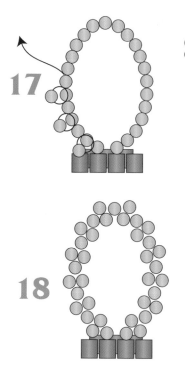

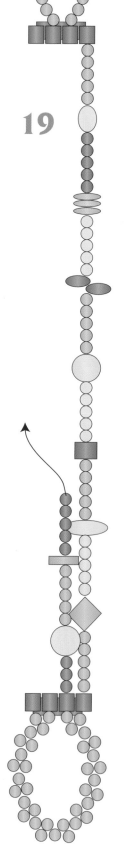

treasure necklace & bracelet
...continued from page 8

To attach the toggle to an end connector, thread your needle with 36" of doubled thread. Tie your thread on a connector and weave until your needle comes out of the second bead from the left on the side with four beads. Pick up 5 Treasure beads and pass your needle through one of the beads in the middle of the toggle. Pick up 5 more Treasure beads and pass your needle down through the third bead from the left of the connector. (Illustration 15)

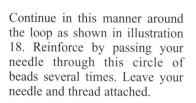

Reinforce the connection by passing through the circle of beads several times. Leave your needle and thread attached and set aside.

To make the beaded loop at the opposite end of the bracelet, thread your needle with 36" of doubled thread. Tie your thread on a connector and weave until your needle comes out of the second bead from the left on the side with four beads. Pick up 25 Treasure beads and pass your needle down through the third bead from the left of the connector. (Illustration 16)

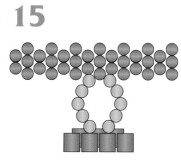

Bring your needle up through the second large Treasure bead from the left. Pick up a small Treasure bead, skip the first Treasure in the loop and pass your needle through the second Treasure in the loop. Pick up another Treasure. Skip the next bead in the loop and pass your needle through the second bead. (Illustration 17)

Continue in this manner around the loop as shown in illustration 18. Reinforce by passing your needle through this circle of beads several times. Leave your needle and thread attached.

Using the needle and thread from the loop connector, thread on 5 Treasure beads and an accent bead. Alternate between 5 Treasures and an accent bead until you reach the desired length. You may need to adjust the bead count between accent beads to accommodate the desired length and to stagger the accent beads along the length of the bracelet.

At the end of a row, pass your needle through the corresponding large bead on the toggle connector, then bring your needle up through the large bead next to it and work back up the bracelet. (Illustration 19) Use the thread from the button end to work some of the rows as well. Add thread as needed to complete your bracelet.

simple scallop necklace

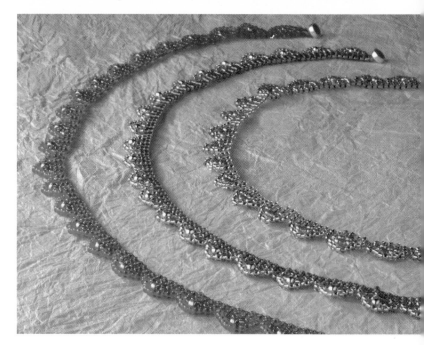

Materials:

Teal & Blue
6 grams 11/0 #23
4 grams 11/0 #274
2 grams 8/0 silver plated

Red
7 grams 11/0 #5
2 grams 11/0 #951
2 grams 8/0 #557

Copper & Purple
7 grams 11/0 #740
2 grams 11/0 #551
2 grams 8/0 #2114

Basic Supplies:
Size B beading thread
Size 12 beading needle
Clasp, Scissors

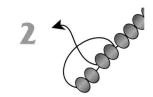

Thread needle with 48" of thread. Pick up a bead and pass through it twice in the same direction (be careful not to split the thread). Leave about a 24" tail. This is the stopper bead. *(Illustration 1)*

Rows 1 & 2:

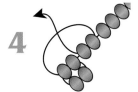

Next we'll make a 2-bead ladder. If you haven't used this method before, it may help to lay your work out on a table until you get used to it. (This ladder can also be used as the base row for brick stitch projects.) Thread on 434 main color Treasure beads. Move them down to within a few inches of the stopper bead.
Take your needle back through the 3rd and 4th bead from the end as shown in illustration 2.

Pull your thread slowly. (The beads on the end will turn over.) Arrange the beads as shown in illustration 3.

Pass your needle back through the next two beads as shown in illustration 4.

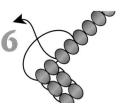

Pull your thread slowly. (The set of four beads will turn over.) Arrange the beads as shown in illustration 5.

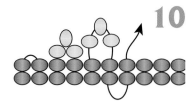

Pass your needle back through the next two beads as shown in illustration 6.

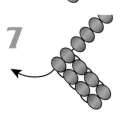

Pull your thread slowly. (The set of six beads will turn over.) Arrange the beads as shown in illustration 7.

Continue in this manner until all the beads have been added to the ladder.
You will have to move the stopper bead farther down the tail from time to time as this method uses thread from both ends.

Row 3:

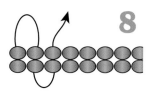

(secondary color)
Position the ladder as shown in illustration 8. Pass the needle down and then up through the next two bead groups. *(Illustration 8)*

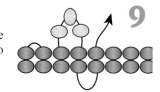

Thread on three beads. Pass the needle down and then up through the next two sets of beads. *(Illustration 9)*

Repeat the stitch using three beads. *(Illustration 10)*
Make sure the three beads are arranged in a pyramid as shown in illustration 10.

Bead across the ladder using this pattern: skip 2 groups, add 3 beads, add 3 beads. *(Illustration 11)*

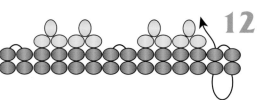

Row 4:

(main color)
Pass your needle up through the second set of beads. *(Illustration 12)*

Continued on page 12

Repeat steps 13 - 15 along the length of the neck-lace. *(Illustration 16)*

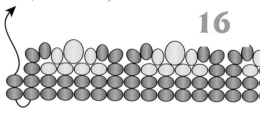

16

Row 5:
(main color). Thread the needle through the last three beads of the previous row as shown. *(Illustration 17)*

17

Thread on 5 beads and pass your needle back down through the next three-bead group of the previous row and the two-bead set. Then pass back up through the next two-bead set and three-bead group as shown in illustration 18.

18

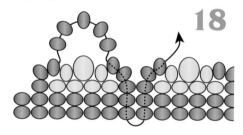

Repeat for the length of the necklace. *(Illustration 19)*

19

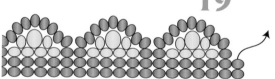

Finishing: Remove the stopper bead. Stitch a split ring to each end of the necklace as shown in illustration 20. Make several passes through the beads and split ring to secure.
Weave the end of thread through several rows of stitching and clip close.
Attach clasp to split rings.

20

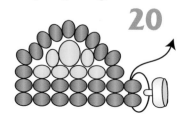

simple scallop necklace
...continued from page 11

13

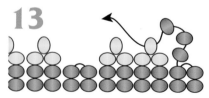

Thread on three beads. Pass your needle through the first "tall" bead of a three-bead pyramid. *(Illustration 13)*

14

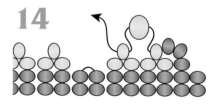

Thread on a size 8/0 bead. Pass your needle through the next "tall" bead. *(Illustration 14)*

15

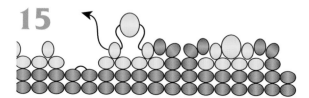

Thread on three beads. Take your needle down and then up through all four beads of the next two groups. *(Illustration 15)*

cube bracelet

Materials:

Copper & Cream
2 grams 8/0 triangles #169
2 grams 8/0 triangles #224
2 grams 8/0 triangles #551
1 gram 8/0 round #34
1 gram 8/0 round #147
1 gram 8/0 round #224
1 gram 8/0 round #552F
1 gram 8/0 round #763

Green
2 grams 8/0 triangle #27B
2 grams 8/0 triangle #167B
2 grams 8/0 triangle #270
2 grams 8/0 triangle #707
1 gram 8/0 round #24BF
1 gram 8/0 round #36
1 gram 8/0 round #507
1 gram 8/0 round #561F

Orange
2 grams 8/0 triangles #30C
2 grams 8/0 triangles #174B
2 grams 8/0 triangles #174C
1.5 grams 8/0 round #802
1.5 grams 8/0 round #803
1.5 grams 8/0 round #2112

Basic Supplies:
10 feet .5mm elastic thread
Tapestry needle
Scissors

Mix three colors of round and triangle beads together into two groups.

Thread your needle with a long section of elastic thread - at least 36" long - the longer the better.

As you work with this thread you might find it wants to stick to itself. Here's a tip - put a little talcum powder on a paper towel. Then run the thread through the towel to coat it lightly with powder.

Row 1: String 4 triangle beads. Pass your needle back through the third bead from the end. *(Illustration 1)* Pull the thread loop until the two beads line up as in illustration 2.

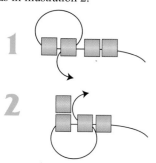

Pass your needle back through the second bead from the end. *(Illustration 2)* Pull the elastic thread loop until the three beads line up with each other as in illustration 3. Don't pull the elastic tight, just enough to hold the beads in place.

Pass your needle back through the last bead. Straighten all the beads so that they look like illustration 4. Now pass the needle through the top bead as shown in illustration 4.

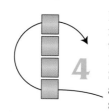

Pull gently but firmly until the beads make two rows of two beads as shown in illustration 5. Tie an overhand knot or two with the end of the elastic thread. Pass your needle back up through the nearest bead as shown in iIllustration 5.

Row 2:
Thread 2 round beads on your thread and pass your needle down through the triangle just to the right of the first one as shown in illustration 6. Bring your needle back up through the next triangle bead to the right. (Triangle beads are represented by squares in these instructions.)

Turn your chain over to begin the next step. The illustrations are shaded to let you know what side of the chain you are working on.

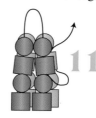

Thread two more round beads and pass the needle down through the next triangle to the right. Bring the needle back up through the top of the first round of beads you added in Row 2. *(Illustration 7)*

Row 3:
Turn your chain over to begin the next step. Thread two triangle beads and pass the needle down through the next round to the right. Bring your needle up through the round to its right. *(Illustration 8)*

Turn your chain over to begin the next step. Thread two triangle beads and pass the needle down through the next triangle to the right. Bring your needle back up through the triangle to its right and the first triangle of the row. *(Illustration 9)*

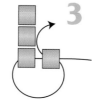

Row 4:
Turn your chain over now to begin the next step. Thread two round beads and pass the needle down through the next triangle to the right. Bring your needle back up through the triangle to its right. *(Illustration 10)*

Turn your chain over to begin next step. Thread two round beads and pass needle down through the next triangle to the right. Bring needle back up through triangle to its right and the first round of row. *(Illustration 11)*

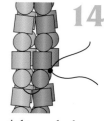

Rows 5 - ?
Repeat steps 9-12 until the bracelet is the desired length. End with a round row.

The classic herringbone effect (when the bead pairs lean into each other) will begin very quickly after Row 3. If you pay attention to the herringbone pattern, you'll know your thread path is right on.

Remember - don't pull your elastic thread tight with every stitch - just enough to move the beads into place.

When you run out of thread, just tie an overhand knot or two with the ends of the elastic and keep going!

Joining the ends:
Think of joining the first row to the last as just another row like you did in steps 10 & 11!
Pass your needle up through the first triangle of the base row. You can recognize it because it's the one with the tail! Take your needle back down through the triangle to its right and through the round just to the right and below of your starting point. *(Illustration 12)*

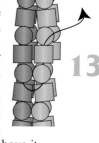

Turn your chain one quarter turn clockwise. Bring your needle back up through the next round and up through the triangle above it. *(Illustration 13)*

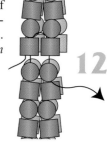

Turn your chain one quarter turn clockwise. Bring needle down through the next triangle to the right and down through the round below it. *(Illustration 14)*

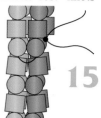

Turn your chain one quarter turn clockwise. Bring your needle up through the next round to the right. Tie the ends of elastic thread with a couple more square knots. Test knots to make sure they hold and weave ends through the chain. *(Illustration 15)*

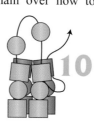

stretch cuff bracelet

Materials:

Black & Grey
3 grams 8/0 #29AF
3 grams 8/0 #566
3 grams 8/0 #611
3 grams 8/0 nickel-plated
3 grams 3.3 Treasure #49
3 grams 3.3 Treasure #610

Blue & Green
3 grams 8/0 #505
3 grams 8/0 #561F
3 grams 8/0 #2010
3 grams 8/0 silver-plated
2.5 grams 3.3 Treasure #601
4 grams 3.3 Treasure #706

Purple
3 grams 8/0 #19F
3 grams 8/0 #166
3 grams 8/0 #705
3 grams 8/0 brass
5 grams 3.3 Treasure #461
2 grams 3.3 Treasure #85

Basic Supplies:
15 feet .5mm Elasticity
2" Big-Eye needle
Scissors

A Note About Colors.
The secret of this bracelet is random rows of color. There is no pattern!

Let's begin.
Thread your needle with a long section of elastic thread at least 36" long but the longer the better.
As you work with this thread you might find it wants to stick to itself. Here's a tip - put a little talcum powder on a paper towel. Then run the thread through the towel to coat it lightly with powder.
Thread on 5 Treasure beads. Move the beads down to the end of the thread leaving a 5" tail.
Pass your needle back through the next to last bead as shown. (Illustration 1)

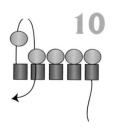

Pull the thread through slowly and arrange the beads as shown in illustration 2.
Pass the needle through the next bead to the right. (Illustration 2)
Pull the thread through slowly and arrange the beads as shown in illustration 3. Pass the needle through the next bead to the right. (Illustration 3)
Pull the thread through slowly and arrange the beads as shown in illustration 4.
Pass your needle through the last bead as shown.
Pull the thread through slowly. Turn the piece on its side and arrange the beads as shown in illustration 5. The ladder is complete. (Illustration 5)

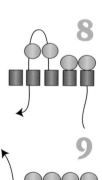

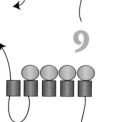

Row 2: Thread on two 8/0 beads and pass your needle down through the next Treasure bead as shown in illustration 6.
Bring your needle back up through the next Treasure bead in the row. (Illustration 7)

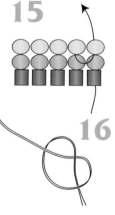

Thread on two 8/0 beads. Pass your needle down through the next Treasure bead in the row. (Illustration 8)

Bring your needle back up through the last Treasure bead on the left. (Illustration 9)

Thread on a single 8/0 and pass your needle down through the fourth 8/0 bead of the row. (Illustration 10)

Bring your needle back up through the 8/0 bead you just added. (Illustration 11)

Row 3:
Thread on two more 8/0 beads. Take your needle down through the next 8/0 in the row and then back up through the bead next to it as shown in illustration 12.
Thread on two more 8/0 beads. Take your needle down through the next 8/0 bead in the row and then back up through the bead next to it as shown in illustration 13.
Thread on a single bead and take your needle down through the fourth bead of the row. (Illustration 14)
Bring your needle back up through the bead you just added. (Illustration 15)

Rows 4 - ??:
Repeat as for Row 3 (alternating bead colors and shapes randomly) until the bracelet is the desired length.
Let's face facts: At some point, you are going to run out of thread. To attach another length of thread, simply place the cut sides together and tie an overhand knot (or two). (Illustration 16)
Weave the tails through several rows of stitching and then cut them close. The knot should be hidden inside a bead or between stitches.
To join the ends of your bracelet simply treat the first row of beads as if it were just another row you were stitching.
Follow the thread path in illustration 17. Tie the ends in an overhand knot (or two) and weave the tails through several rows of stitching before cutting them close.

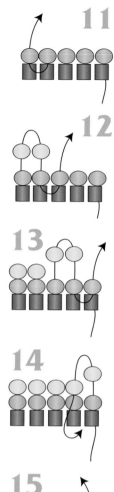

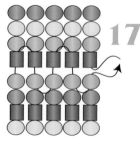

multi-strand
necklace & bracelets

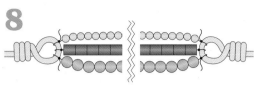

Tie the loose end of the threads securely around one of the wrapped loops. Thread on the first strand of beads. Tie the other end of the strand securely to the second wrapped loop. Tie each strand of beads to the wrapped loops in this manner. As the bead strands accumulate on the loops, you may have to add a few beads to the later strands to accomodate the bulk. *(Illustration 8)*

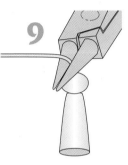

Thread the end of one wrapped loop through the large end of a cone. Thread on an 8/0 bead and grasp the wire with your pliers about $1/8"$ from the end of the jaws. Bend the wire at a 90ß angle. *(Illustration 9)*

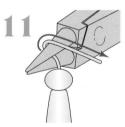

Pivot your pliers from horizontal to vertical just as you did earlier. *(Illustration 10)*

1

Cut a 4" long piece of 22 gauge wire. Grasp the wire with your round-nose pliers about $1^1/4"$ from the top. Bend the wire at a 90ß angle. *(Illustration 1)*

2

Let your grip loosen on the pliers and pivot them from horizontal to vertical. Apply pressure to the pliers again when your work looks like illustration 2.

3

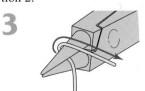

Wrap the short piece of wire over the top jaw of the pliers as shown in illustration 3.

Reposition the wire on the bottom jaw of the pliers. *(Illustration 4)*

4

5

ers. *(Illustration 5)*
Remove the loop and hold it in place as shown in illustration 6.
Without touching the long end of the wire, begin coiling the shorter piece of wire around the

6

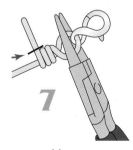

7

longer piece.
Begin your coils as close to the loop as possible. Make two or three coils then clip the end of wire close to the coils as shown in illustration 7. Repeat steps 1 through 7 for a second wrapped loop.
Thread your needle with 72" of doubled thread. Wax the thread so that the thread sticks together. Determine the length of your necklace or bracelet. Subtract 1" for the length of the clasp. This is the length of each strand of beads.

Complete the loop by wrapping the short end of the wire around the bottom jaw of the pli-

Wrap the wire around the top jaw of your pliers as shown in illustration 11.

11

Move the piece to the bottom jaw of the pliers and complete the loop as shown in illustration 12.

12

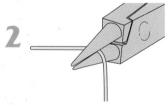

Open the loop up a bit and thread on one half of the 2-part clasp or lobster claw clasp. Complete the wrapped loop. Repeat with other half of 2-part clasp or closed ring on the other end. *(Illustration 13)*

13

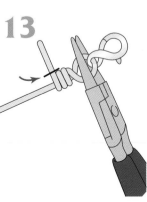

Materials:

Pink Bracelet

7.5 grams 8/0 hex #960	*2
3 grams 8/0 #959	*1
5.5 grams 8/0 #166	*2
5 grams 8/0 #563F	*2
3.5 grams 11/0 #515F	*2
2 grams 11/0 #515F	*1

Sea Green Bracelet

4 grams 8/0 hex #144	*1
3 grams 8/0 #561F	*1
3 grams 8/0 #572	*1
3 grams 8/0 #805	*1
2 grams 11/0 #954	*1
4 grams 11/0 #975	*2

White 18" Necklace

4 grams 8/0 triangle #161	*2
6 grams 8/0 #761	*2
6.5 grams 8/0 #121	*2
7 grams 8/0 hex #141	*2
5 grams 8/0 #551	*2
4 grams 11/0 #1	*2
3.5 grams 11/0 #41	*2
3 grams 11/0 #101	*2
10 grams 11/0 #141	*2
4.5 grams 11/0 #161F	*2
2 grams 11/0 #551	*2

Findings:

2 small bead cones
Beading needle
Size D beading thread
8" of 22 gauge
   sterling wire
Toggle clasp or lobster
   claw clasp and
   closed ring

Basic Supplies:

Round-nose pliers

* number of bracelet or
   necklace strands

wide-edge bracelet

Designed by Mary Voth

Materials:

Red & Gold
2.5 grams 11/0 hex #22BF
2 grams 11/0 #25CF
3 grams 11/0 triangle #22
7 grams 8/0 #25C

Seafoam
2.5 grams 11/0 hex #706
2 grams 11/0 #561
3 grams 11/0 triangle #706
7 grams 8/0 #561F

Slate Grey & Blue
2.5 grams 11/0 hex #49
2 grams 11/0 #588
3 grams 11/0 triangle #511F
7 grams 8/0 #565

Basic Supplies:
Shank button for clasp
Size 10 or 12 beading needle
Beading thread
Scissors

Spacers:
Thread your needle with 48" of thread. Pick up a bead and pass through it twice in the same direction (be careful

not to split the thread). Leave a 12" tail as shown in illustration 1. This is called the stopper bead and it is there to prevent the working beads from coming off the end of the thread.

Thread on an 11/0, an 11/0 hex and another 11/0 bead. Move the beads down to the end of the thread against the stopper bead. Add another set of beads just like the first. Pass your needle back up through the first set of beads and then down through the second set as shown in illustration 2.

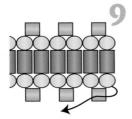

Add another set of beads and pass the needle down through the second set and back up through the third set as shown in illustration 3.

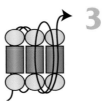

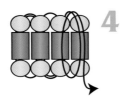

Add another set of beads. Pass the needle up through the third set and back down through the fourth set as shown in illustration 4.

Continue to add the sets of beads in this manner until your bracelet measures 3/4" less than the desired length. *(Illustration 5)*

Note: Your bracelet must have an even number of sets.

Row 2: Thread on an 11/0 triangle bead. Pass your needle down through the next group, add another 11/0 triangle. Pass your needle up through the last group, the first 11/0 triangle and the next to last group. *(Illustration 6)*

Pass your needle back up through the next row.

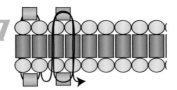

Thread on an 11/0 triangle. Pass your needle down through the next group. Add an 11/0 triangle. Pass your needle back up through the previous group, through the 11/0 triangle and back down the next group. *(Illustration 7)*

Repeat steps 6 and 7 across the bracelet as shown in illustration 8.

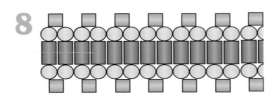

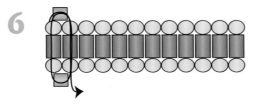

At the end of row, pass needle back through second 11/0 triangle added. *(Illustration 9)*

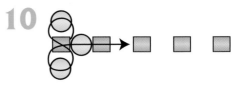

You'll now be working the top edge of the bracelet. Illustration 10 is the view looking down on the top edge. Thread on an 8/0 bead. Pass your needle back through the 11/0 triangle from right to left. Add another 8/0 bead. Pass your needle through the 11/0 triangle from left to right. Add another 8/0 bead and pass your needle through the next 11/0 triangle as shown in illustration 10.

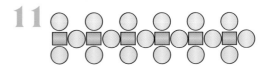

Continue adding 8/0 beads along the top edge of the bracelet. *(Illustration 11)*

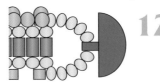

When you reach the end of the row, you'll add the button for the clasp. Thread on five 11/0 beads, the button and five more 11/0 beads. *(Illustration 12)*

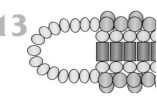

Pass your needle through the first 11/0 triangle on the bottom edge and add 8/0s as before to the end of the row.

When you reach the opposite end of the bracelet, thread on a loop of 11/0 beads large enough to accomodate your button. *(Illustration 13)*

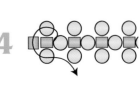

Thread your needle through the 11/0 triangle and then pass your needle from right to left through one of the 8/0 beads at the end of the bracelet. Thread on an 11/0 triangle. Pass your needle through the 8/0 on the other side of the top edge as shown in illustration 14.

Continue to add an 11/0 triangle between each of the 8/0s around the top edge of the bracelet. *(Illustration 15)*

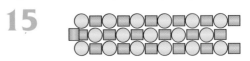

Weave your needle down to the bottom edge and repeat steps 14 and 15 to complete the bottom edge of the bracelet.

Thread on two more seed beads. Position them so that they rest on top of the last two beads of Row 1. *(Illustration 2)*

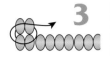

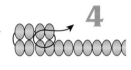

Pass the needle through the last two beads of Row 1 and the two new beads as shown in Illustration 3.

Thread two more beads. Pass the needle through the next two beads of Row 1 and the two new beads. *(Illustration 4)*

Continue to work two beads per stitch until you get to the size 6/0 beads. Pass your needle through all three size 6/0 beads. Thread on a pair of seed beads and make another stitch. *(Illustration 5)*

You're doing just fine!
Try to keep your tension consistent and the pairs of beads as close together as possible.

Usually square stitch is done with single beads but we're doubling up because it's faster and forms a nice grid pattern. Pairs are also easier to count, helping you keep your place.
Stitch 18 pairs of beads. Pass your needle through the three 8/0 beads, then continue stitching pairs of beads to the end of the row. *(Illustration 6)*

Take a look at your bracelet. Not too bad, huh? It may be bowed out along the side of the new stitching. Not to worry. Remember that stopper bead we tied on at the beginning? Loosen it up a bit and let the tension out of the first row. You can almost hear your bracelet say "aahhh"! Straighten out the rows as much as possible, trying to make sure the "fun stuff" is centered between the rows of stitching.

Continued on page 24

fun stuff bracelet

We start with a stopper bead!
Thread your needle with 48" of thread. Pick up a bead and pass through it twice in the same direction (be careful not to split the thread). Leave a 6" tail as shown in illustration 1.

Measure your wrist with a tape measure and determine the size you wish your bracelet to be.

Row 1: (right to left on diagram below)
Thread on:
46 seed beads
3 size 8/0 beads (your choice of color)
36 seed beads
3 size 6/0 beads (your choice of color)
now thread on the correct number of seed beads based on the size of your bracelet

6 1/2"	22 seed beads
7"	30 seed beads
7 1/2"	38 seed beads
8"	46 seed beads

Row 2: (left to right on diagram below)
Be careful, that stopper bead is meant to keep the beads from sliding off the thread, but that's not a guarantee.

three 8/0 hex
or one

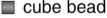

☐ cylinder bead   ▭ thin cathedral   ○ 8/0 bead   ■ cube bead   ○ 6/0 bead

8"   7½"   7"   6½"

Materials:

Burgundy
10 grams 11/0 #703
12 grams 6/0 #22
10 grams 3.3 Treasures #332
6 grams 8/0 hex #406
12 grams 8/0 #564F
15 grams 8/0 #203
6 grams 6/0 #224
52 grams 15/0 #221
4 grams 4mm cubes #610
8 grams 4mm cubes #166
2 thin cathedral beads

Forest
10 grams 11/0 #37
12 grams 6/0 #504
6 grams 3.3 Treasures #85
6 grams 8/0 hex #406
4 grams 8/0 #19
12 grams 8/0 #166D
15 grams 8/0 #39F
6 grams 6/0 #940
52 grams 15/0 #221
4 grams 4mm cubes #86
8 grams 4mm cubes #39
2 thin cathedral beads
52 15/0 #6C

Blue & Silver
10 grams 11/0 #511F
18 grams 6/0 #21
10 grams 3.3 Treasures #711
4 grams 8/0 hex #288
15 grams 8/0 #29AF
12 grams 8/0 #558
4 grams 4mm cubes #566
8 grams 4mm cubes #82
2 thin cathedral beads
52 15/0 #711

Basic Supplies:
2 small buttons for clasp
Beading thread
Size 10 or 12 beading needle
Scissors

15/0 bead

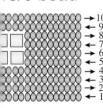

fun stuff bracelet
...continued from
page 22

pairs and thread on 2 more cubes. Work the next three pairs of beads then thread on two cylinder beads. Skip the next two pairs then work two more pairs. Thread on three 6/0s, work three more pairs and thread on five 8/0s (new color). Skip over 4 pairs.

6½" and 7" bracelets: work to the end of the row.

7½" and 8" bracelets: work four pairs of beads, thread on a cathedral bead and work to the end of the row.

Row 6: (left to right on diagram - page 22)
Work across the row, passing the needle through all of the "fun stuff" (except the 15/0s which have their own row).

Row 7: (right to left on diagram - page 22) Work across the row until you reach the 15/0 group. Thread on 8 seed beads to span across the top of the section. (Illustration 14)

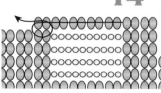

7

Row 3: (right to left on diagram - page 22) Add two seed beads and make a stitch in the opposite direction. (Illustration 7)

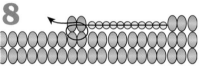

8

After you've worked 12 pairs of beads, thread on thirteen size 15/0 beads and then two 11/0 beads. Skip over 4 pairs of beads on Row 2 and work a stitch in fifth pair. (Illustration 8)

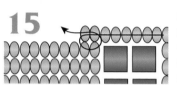

14

Continue to work across the row until you reach the group of 4mm cubes. Thread 6 beads to span the top of that section. (Illustration 15)

15

9

Work 6 more pairs of beads until you come to the 8/0s. Thread on three 8/0s and two 11/0s and work a stitch in the next pair of 11/0s from Row 2. (Illustration 9)

All of the "fun stuff" (except the 15/0s) will be centered between two rows of stitching.

6½" and 7" bracelets: work to the end of the row.

7½" & 8" bracelets: refer to illustrations 14 & 15 and span 4 seed beads across the top of the cathedral bead or 8/0 hex beads.

7½" bracelets: work to the end of the row.

8" bracelets only: Work 3 pairs of beads, thread on 2 cylinder beads, skip over 2 pairs of beads and work to the end of the row.

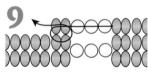

10

Work 8 pairs of beads. Thread on two cube beads. Skip over three pairs of beads on Row 2 and make a stitch in the fourth pair. (Illustration 10)

Rows 8 - 10: Refer to diagram on front page to complete these rows. **Once more with feeling** Pass your needle back through every row to reinforce and if needed to even out the stitching.

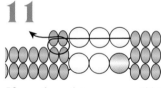

11

Work over to the set of three 6/0 beads. Thread on three 6/0 beads and two 11/0s. Work a stitch in the next pair of 11/0 seed beads from Row 2. (Illustration 11)

If your bracelet measures 6½" or 7" long, continue to stitch pairs of beads to the end of the row.

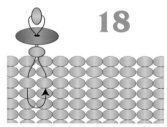

16

Button and Loop Closure
Weave needle through end of bracelet as shown. String 12 seed beads and pass needle back up through the bead to its right. (Illustration 16)
Run thread through beaded loop again to strengthen.

7½" and 8" bracelets only:
Work 11 pairs of seed beads. Thread on a thin cathedral bead (any color) and two 11/0 beads. Skip over two pairs of beads on Row 2. Make a stitch in the next pair. (Illustration 12)
Continue to stitch pairs of beads to the end of the row.

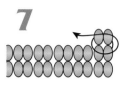

12

Weave needle through end of bracelet as shown. Thread on 12 seed beads and pass needle back up through the bead to its right. (Illustration 17) Run thread through beaded loop again.

17

13

Row 4: (left to right on diagram page 22) Work across the row, passing the needle through the chicklet (if applicable), 6/0s, cubes and 8/0s. When you come to the 15/0s, thread on 13 beads, then work pairs of 11/0s to the end of the row. (Illustration 13)

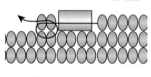

18

Pass needle up through the length of the third row of bracelet emerging as shown in illustration 18. Thread a seed bead, a black disk and a seed bead. Pass the needle back through the disk and first seed bead coming down through the bead just to the left of the exit bead. Pass thread through button assembly once more.

Row 5: (right to left on diagram - page 22)
Work the first five pairs of the row. Thread on four 4mm cubes, skip the next five pairs of beads then work two more stitches. Thread on 13 size 15/0 beads. Work the next three pairs and thread on two 6/0s (new color). Skip over the next two pairs of beads. Work the next two pairs and thread on three 8/0s. Work 8

Weave needle through beads along short edge of bracelet to opposite side. Assemble another button. (Illustration 19) Reinforce button. Weave thread through several stitches before clipping end. Remove stopper bead and do the same for the thread tail.

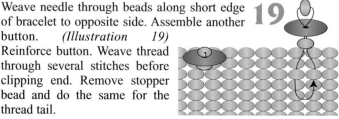

19

business card case

Materials:
Pink, Purple & Blue
20 grams 11/0 #26
20 grams 11/0 #3B
12 grams 11/0 #563
Fig
52 grams 11/0 #224

Basic Supplies:
Snap-on jean repair button
30mm Black stone donut
4 black 11/0 beads
Beading thread
Size 10 or 12 beading needle
Scissors

We start with a stopper bead!

Thread needle with 48" of thread. Pick up a bead and pass through it twice in the same direction (be careful not to split the thread). Leave a 24" tail. Be sure to leave a 24" tail. We'll be needing it very soon.
(Illustration 1)

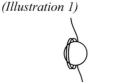

Rows 1 & 2:

Next we'll make a 2-bead ladder. If you haven't used this method before, it may help to lay your work out on a table until you get used to it. (This ladder can also be used as the base row for brick stitch projects.) Thread on 120 beads. Move them down to within a few inches of the stopper bead.

Take your needle back through the 3rd and 4th bead from the end as shown in Illustration 2.

Pull your thread slowly. (The beads on the end will turn over.) Arrange the beads as shown in illustration 3.

Pass your needle back through the next two beads as shown in illustration 4.

Pull your thread slowly. (The set of four beads will turn over.) Arrange the beads as shown in illustration 5.

Pass your needle back through the next two beads as shown in illustration 6. Pull your thread slowly. (The set of six beads will turn over.) Arrange the beads as shown in illustration 7. Continue in this manner until all the beads have been added to the ladder.

You will have to move the stopper bead farther down the tail from time to time as this method uses thread from both ends.

When you have completed the ladder, join the last set of beads with the first as shown in illustration 8.

Row 3: Thread on two beads. Pass your needle down through the first bead group of the ladder and then up through the second group of two beads.
(Illustration 9)

Thread on two more beads. Pass your needle down and then up through the next two beads groups.
(Illustration 10)
Continue stitching in this manner.

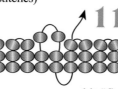

Completing the Row:

When you have worked around the row (60 beads, 30 stitches) bring your needle up through the first two-bead group **and** the first bead of Row 3 as shown in illustration 11.

Note: These next few rows may seem a bit "floppy". Don't worry, keep working - the pattern will start to take shape and your stitches will fall into place very soon.

Row 4:

Thread on two beads. Pass your needle down through the second bead of Row 3 and then back up through the third bead. *(Illustration 12)*

Thread on two more beads. Pass your needle down and then up through the next two beads of the previous row. *(Illustration 13)* Continue to add two beads with every stitch.

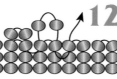

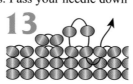

Completing the Row:

When you have worked around the row (60 beads, 30 stitches) bring your needle up through the first bead of Row 3 **and** the first bead of Row 4 as shown in illustration 14. (You'll end every row in this manner.)

Rows 5-39:

Work as for Row 4. Sounds simple enough, but at some point you'll start wondering why you ever wanted to make this project. In fact you'll think about a lot of things...like the pyramids. Or the Great Wall of China.

To Add New Thread:

When you come to within 6" or so of thread remaining, weave it back down through several stitches to secure. Cut a new length of thread and weave it up through several rows (follow the thread paths) eventually bringing your needle back up through the last stitch you added.

Row 40: (We're using black beads to mark a space on the front of the case for the button back.) Make a stitch with one regular and one black bead.
(Illustration 15)

Make the second stitch with a black bead and a regular bead.
(Illustration 16) Work the rest of row as usual.

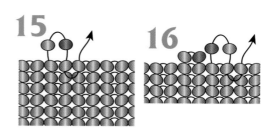

Continued on page 26

Row 41:
Work as for Row 40.
(*Illustration 17*)

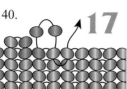

Row 42:
Work the first stitch as shown in illustration 18. (Work this first stitch loosely. We're leaving a space between the stitching for the button back to poke through.) Now stitch the rest of the row as usual.

Rows 43-53: Work as for Row 4. Work the next row **without** beads as shown in Illustration 19. This step completes Row 53 and gives a nicer finish to the top edge of the case. Weave the end of the thread down through several rows of stitching to secure. Clip close.

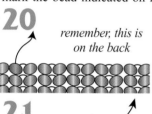

Let's make the flap. Fold your piece in half so that the black beads are centered on the front. Turn the piece over to the **back** and mark the bead indicated on illustration 20 with a bit of thread or nail polish (anything that makes it easy to find later.) Thread your needle with a new length of thread. Weave it up through several rows of stitching eventually bringing your needle out through marked bead.

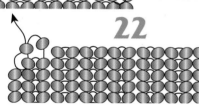

remember, this is on the back

Row 1:
Work 13 stitches (26 beads). Work the next stitch as shown in illustration 21. 14 stitches total in the row.

Row 2: Working in the opposite direction, make 13 stitches across the row. Work the next stitch as shown in illustration 22. 14 stitches total in the row.

Rows 3 - 14: Work as for Rows 1 and 2.

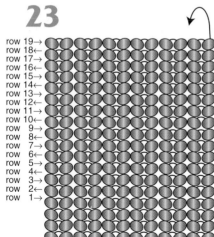

row 19→
row 18←
row 17→
row 16←
row 15→
row 14←
row 13→
row 12←
row 11→
row 10←
row 9→
row 8←
row 7→
row 6←
row 5→
row 4←
row 3→
row 2←
row 1→

Buttonhole (left side): Work 19 rows. 6 stitches (12 beads) per row. Weave end of thread through several rows of stitching to secure. Clip close.
Buttonhole (right side): Begin new thread at bead marked below. Work 20 rows. Do not clip thread. (*Illustration 24*)

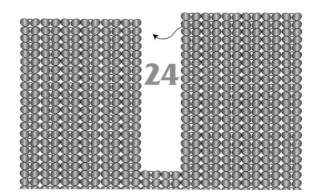

Finish Buttonhole:
Thread on two beads. Pass your needle down through the last two beads on the right side of the buttonhole then up through the new beads. (*Illustrations 25 & 26*)

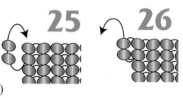

Thread on two more beads. Pass your needle up through the two beads you just added and then down through the new beads.

Thread on two more beads. Pass your needle up through the two beads you just added and then down through the new beads. (*Illustrations 27 & 28*) Add two more sets of beads in this manner. (*Illustrations 29 & 30*)

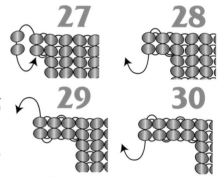

Join the new section to the other half of the buttonhole as shown in Illustration 30. Continue stitching as before across the row.
Turn and stitch 6 more complete rows.

Stitch one more row across the flap without beads just as you did for the body. (*Illustration 32*)

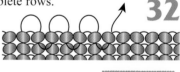

Go back and reinforce the outside edges of the buttonhole. Run your thread along the long edges and weave through the short sides several times. This part of the case will receive a lot of wear and tear and you want to make it as strong as possible - especially the corners. Reinforce the black bead section on the front of the case as well. Run your thread loosely around (not between) those four beads a few times to strengthen that section.

Stitch up the bottom of the case. Fold the case in half, centering the black beads on the front. Start with the second ladder from the end. (You'll be going through 2 bead groups because this row was the original 2-bead ladder.) Thread on 2 new beads and pass the needle through the second ladder from the end on the opposite side. Bring the needle back up through the ladder next to it. Continue in this manner across the bottom of the case. (*Illustrations 33 & 34*)

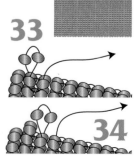

Attaching the Button. Open up the case and very carefully poke the button back out between black beads on front. (You don't want to break a thread right now!) Place the stone donut over the point and then slowly press button front onto the point. A gentle even pressure is all that's needed. Once the button is pressed into place it will not come off without damaging the beadwork.

wheels bracelet

Designed by Megan Lauch

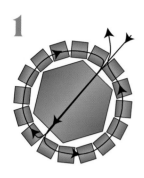

Row 1:

String one fire polish bead and 8 Treasure beads. Take the needle through the fire polish. String 8 more Treasures and go through fire polish again. Secure your circle of Treasures by going through the fire polish several times as shown in illustration 1. Tie the row off in a double knot.

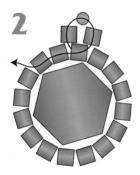

Row 2:

Exit through a Treasure bead and thread on a new color Treasure, a 15/0 and another new color Treasure. Pass the needle back through the original Treasure and two more Treasures from Row 1. *(Illustration 2)*

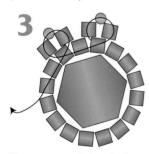

Repeat around the circle as shown in illustration 3.

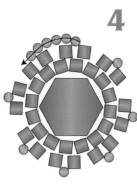

Row 3:

Pass your needle back through the first Treasure and 15/0 of Row 2. Thread on three or four 15/0s and pass your needle through the next 15/0 of Row 2. *(Illustration 4)*

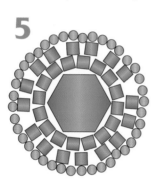

The key to this row is making sure the 15/0s lay flat and no thread shows between the beads. Continue adding 15/0s around the circle. *(Illustration 5)* Reinforce by going back through all the beads of the row.

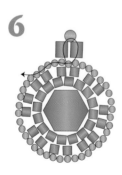

Row 4:

Thread through the first 15/0 of Row 3. Thread on an 11/0 triangle, an 11/0 and another 11/0 triangle. Pass your needle through the original 15/0 and then through four or five 15/0s. *(Illustration 6)*

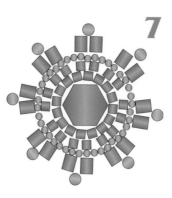

Repeat around the circle to complete the row as shown in illustration 7.

Once again, the key is to make the beads lay flat with no thread showing.

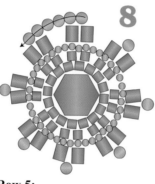

Row 5:

Pass your needle back through the first 11/0 triangle and 11/0 of Row 4. Thread on 4 or 5 11/0s and pass your needle through the next 11/0 of Row 4. *(Illustration 8)*

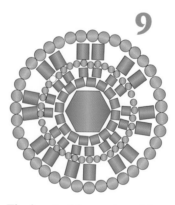

The key to this row is making sure the 11/0s lay flat and no thread shows between the beads. Continue adding 11/0s around the circle. *(Illustration 9)*

Reinforce by going back through all beads of the row. Repeat steps 1 - 9 for as many wheels as it takes to make your bracelet the desired length - usually 6 -7 wheels.

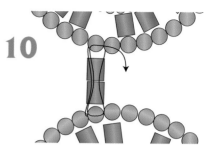

Attaching the wheels:

Line up the wheels so that the fire polish beads are facing in the same direction. Bring your needle out of an 11/0 bead, thread on 2 11/0 triangles and pass your needle through the corresponding bead on the other wheel. Pass your needle through the next bead on the second wheel. *(Illustration 10)*

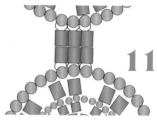

Repeat the process two more times until you have three sets of triangle beads connecting the wheels. *(Illustration 11)*

Pass your thread around the outside of the wheel to the opposite side. Position the next wheel with the fire polish facing in the same direction and connect it to the previous wheel following illustrations 10 and 11. Repeat for all wheels.

Toggle: Rows 1 & 2

Thread your needle with 24" of thread. String 14 small Treasure beads. Thread on another bead. Skip over one bead and pass your needle through the second bead in the row. *(Illustration 12)*

Thread on another bead. Skip over a bead and pass your needle through the next bead in the row. *(Illustration 13)* Complete the row by stitching the remaining 5 beads.

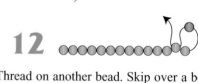

Notice how the beads from the first row "share" the space with the new beads. *(Illustration 14)*

Materials:

Green
1 gram Treasure #167
1.5 grams Treasure #796
1 gram 15/0 #322
2 grams 11/0 triangle #36
3 grams 11/0 #167BF

Wine
1 gram Treasure #703
1.5 grams Treasure #332
1 gram 15/0 #332
2 grams 11/0 triangle #502
3 grams 11/0 #332

Blue
1 gram Treasure #917
1.5 grams Treasure #28
1 gram 15/0 #28
2 grams 11/0 triangle #8
3 grams 11/0 #8

Basic Supplies:
6mm fire polish beads
Size B beading thread
Size 12 beading needle

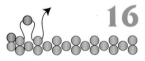

15

Row 3:
Reverse direction. Thread on a bead and pass your needle through the first "tall" bead of the row as shown. *(Illustration 15)*

16

Add a bead between each of the "tall" beads of the row as shown in illustration 16.

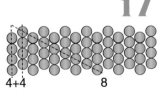

17

4+4   8

Rows 4 - 8:
Continue to add beads in this manner until you have a total of 8 rows. Peyote stitch is counted on the diagonal. An easier way to count is to add 2 columns. Both methods are shown above in illustration 17.

18

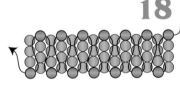

Fold the ends together and you'll notice that they fit together like the teeth of a zipper. Stitch the two ends together. Illustration 18 shows you what that looks like if the piece were flat. Weave the ends of your thread through the beaded piece until they are secure. Clip the ends close.

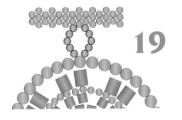

19

To attach the toggle to a wheel, bring your needle out of the top bead of the last wheel. Pick up 5 Treasure beads and pass your needle through one of the beads in the middle of the toggle. Pick up 5 more Treasure beads and pass your needle back through the top bead. *(Illustration 19)*
Reinforce the connection by passing through the circle of beads several times.

To make the beaded loop at the opposite end of the bracelet, bring your needle out of the top bead of the wheel on the opposite side. Pick up 25 Treasure beads and pass your needle back through the top bead *(Illustration 20)*

Pick up a Treasure bead, skip the first Treasure in the loop and pass your needle through the second Treasure in the loop. Pick up another Treasure. Skip the next bead in the loop and pass your needle through the second bead. *(Illustration 21)*

Continue in this manner around the loop. Make sure the beads "share" the space as they did when you were stitching the toggle as shown in illustration 22. Reinforce by passing your needle through this circle of beads several times.

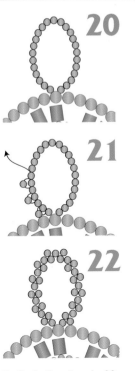

20

21

22

Rows 4 - 8:
Continue to add beads in this manner until you have a total of 8 rows. Peyote stitch is counted on the diagonal. An easier way to count is to add 2 columns. Both methods are shown in illustration 7.

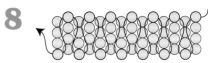

4+4   8

Fold the ends together and you'll notice that they fit together like the teeth of a zipper. Stitch the two ends together.

Illustration 8 shows you what that looks like if the piece were flat. Weave the ends of your

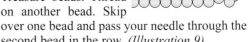

thread through the beaded piece until they are secure. Clip the ends close.

Odd Count Base
Rows 1 & 2:
String an odd number of Treasure beads. Thread on another bead. Skip over one bead and pass your needle through the second bead in the row. (Illustration 9)

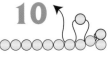

Thread on another bead. Skip over a bead and pass your needle through the next bead in the row. (Illustration 10)

Complete the row by stitching the remaining beads. Pass the needle through the last two beads of the row. Add a bead and then make a figure eight pattern as shown in illustrations 11 & 12.

Row 3:
Reverse direction. Thread on a bead and pass your needle through the next "tall" bead of the row as shown. (Illustration 13)

Add a bead between each of the "tall" beads of the row as shown in illustration 14.

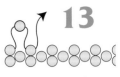

Row 4 :
Reverse direction and add beads between each of the tall beads of the row as shown in illustration 15.

zip beads bracelet
Designed by Marilou Porth

Each of the embellished beads is made over a peyote tube base. There are two types of base bead: one made with an even number of beads and another made with an odd number.

Thread your needle with 36" of thread. Pass your needle through a bead twice (be careful not to split the thread). Leave a 6" tail.

This bead is called a stop bead. It is used to keep the working beads from falling off the end of the thread. (Illustration 1)

2

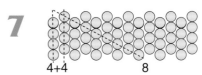

Even Count Base
Rows 1 & 2:
String an even number of Treasure beads. Thread on another bead. Skip over one bead and pass your needle through the second bead in the row. (Illustration 2)

3 Thread on another bead. Skip over a bead and pass your needle through the next bead in the row. (Illustration 3)

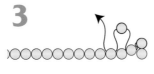

Complete the row by stitching the remaining beads in the same manner. (Illustration 4)

4

Notice how the beads from the first row "share" the space with the new beads?

Row 3:
Reverse direction. Thread on a bead and pass your needle through the first "tall" bead of the row as shown. (Illustration 5)

5

Add a bead between each of the "tall" beads of the row as shown in illustration 6.

6

Sherbet
1 gram 3.3 Treasure #903
2 grams 1.8 Treasure #775
2 grams 1.8 Treasure #780
2 grams 1.8 Treasure #903
2 grams 1.8 Treasure #905
2 grams 1.8 Treasure #906

Browns & Golds
1 gram 3.3 Treasure #702
2 grams 1.8 Treasure #85F
2 grams 1.8 Treasure #278
2 grams 1.8 Treasure #501
2 grams 1.8 Treasure #502
2 grams 1.8 Treasure #557

Teal
1 gram 3.3 Treasure #601
2 grams 1.8 Treasure #7BD
2 grams 1.8 Treasure #23
2 grams 1.8 Treasure #506
2 grams 1.8 Treasure #566
2 grams 1.8 Treasure #711

Basic Supplies:
Toggle clasp
18-20 Bali 5mm or 6mm
  daisy spacers
Size 12 beading needle
Size B beading thread
2 crimp beads or
  crimp tubes
12" of .015 flexible
  beading wire

Rows 5 - 8:
Repeat Rows 3 and 4 until you have a total of 8 rows. Peyote stitch is counted on the diagonal. An easier way to count is to add 2 columns. Both methods are shown in illustration 16.

16

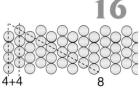

4+4   8

Fold the ends together and stitch the two ends together. Illustration 17 shows you what the finished tube looks like. Weave the ends of your thread through the beaded piece until they are secure. Clip the ends close.

17

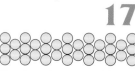

Continued on page 32

zip beads bracelet
...continued from page 31

Polka Dot Bead - Even Count

Begin with an even count tube bead of 10 beads and 8 rows. If you look at the bead closely, you can plainly see the rows of beads. Pass your needle through two of the outside beads of the tube and peyote stitch 3 beads.

Bring your needle through the last two beads of the tube and back through two more beads on the next row. *(Illustrations 1 & 2)*

1

2

Continue to peyote stitch the three center beads of each row until you have added beads to each of the 8 rows. *(Illustrations 3 & 4)*

3

4

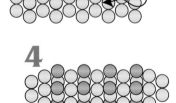

Polka Dot Bead - Odd Count

Begin with an odd count tube bead of 11 beads and 10 rows. If you look at the bead closely, you can plainly see the rows of beads. Pass your needle through two of the outside beads of the tube and peyote stitch 4 beads.
Bring your needle through the last two beads of the tube. Weave through the last bead of the next row and then peyote stitch 4 more beads. Continue to peyote stitch the four center beads of every other row until you have added 5 rows of beads.

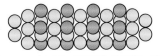

Layered Bead - Even Count

Begin with an even count tube bead of 10 beads and 8 rows. If you look at the bead closely, you can plainly see the rows of beads. Pass your needle through two of the outside beads of the tube as shown in illustration 1 and peyote stitch 3 beads. Reverse direction and work even count flat peyote out from the tube for 20 rows. *(Illustrations 2 & 3)*

1

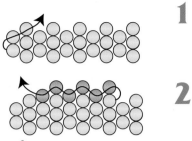

2

3

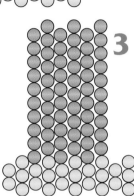

Wrap the flat peyote piece around the tube as shown in illustration 4. Join the ends as you did for the original tube.

4

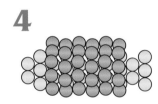

5

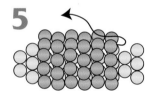

Work your needle over two beads from the edge of the new piece *(Illustration 5)* and peyote stitch one bead. Reverse direction and work even count flat peyote out from the tube for 32 rows. *(Illustrations 6 & 7)*

6

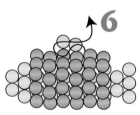

7

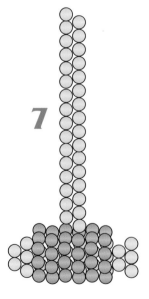

8

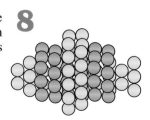

Wrap the flat peyote piece around the tube as shown in illustration 8. Join the ends as you did for the original tube.

tussy mussy necklace

Designed by
Marilou Porth

Basic Supplies:
Clasp
Beading thread
Beading needle
Thread conditioner
Scissors

Materials:
Lavender
5 grams 4mm cube beads #566
5 grams 1.8 Treasures #566
2 grams 8/0 #935
2 grams 8/0 #201
2 grams 11/0 beads #2108
2 grams 11/0 beads #252
2 grams 11/0 beads #26F
100 accent beads (leaf, dagger, bud, etc.) in various shapes and sizes from size 8/0 to 6mm fire polish

Primary Colors
5 grams 4mm cube beads #566
5 grams 1.8 Treasures #566
4 grams 11/0 beads #49
4 grams 11/0 beads #610
100 accent beads (leaf, dagger, bud, etc.) in various shapes and sizes from size 8/0 to 6mm fire polish

Brick Stitch
Brick stitch has a natural decrease. Every row will automatically have 1 less bead or set of beads than the previous row.

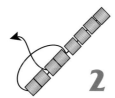

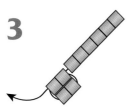

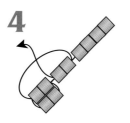

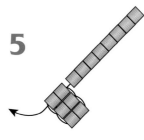

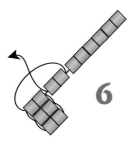

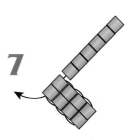

Row 1: Thread your needle with 72" of thread. Double the thread and wax it so the 2 strands stick together. Pick up a bead and pass through it twice in the same direction (be careful not to split the thread). Leave a 12" tail. This bead is called a stop bead and is meant to keep your work from falling off the end of your thread. It will be removed later. Next we'll make a 2-bead ladder. Thread on 14 cube beads. Move them down to the stop bead. Take your needle back through the 3rd and 4th bead from the end as shown in illustration 2.

Pull your thread slowly. (The beads on the end will turn over.) Arrange the beads as shown in illustration 3.

Pass your needle back through the next two beads as shown in illustration 4. Pull your thread slowly. (The set of four beads will turn over.)

Arrange the beads as shown in illustration 5.

Pass your needle back through the next two beads as shown in illustration 6.

Pull your thread slowly. (The set of six beads will turn over.) Arrange the beads as shown in illustration 7.

Continue in this manner until all 14 beads have been added to the ladder (7 groups of two beads). You will have to move the stopper bead farther down the tail from time to time as this method uses thread from both ends.

Row 2: Position the ladder as shown in illustration 8.

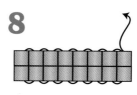

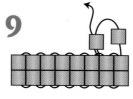

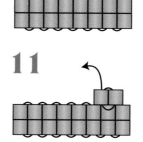

String 2 cube beads. Notice the loops connecting each group of beads across the top edge of Row 1. Skip the loop just next to the thread and hook the needle under the second loop. Bring the needle back up through the last bead. *(Illustration 9)*

Pass the needle back down through the first set of beads, catch the first loop of thread, and then bring the needle back up through the second set. *(Illustrations 10 & 11)*

Continued on page 34

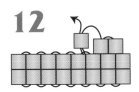

12

This "locks" the first group of beads to the second and keeps it in line with the rest of the row. String a bead, hook needle under the next loop and bring needle back up through bead.
(Illustration 12)

13

Work 4 more beads across the row. You should have 7 beads in this second row.
(Illustration 13)

14

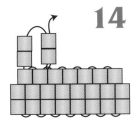

Row 3: String 4 cube beads. Skip the loop just next to the thread and hook the needle under the second loop. Bring the needle back up through the last two beads as shown in illustration 14.

15

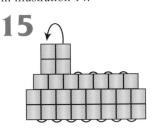

16

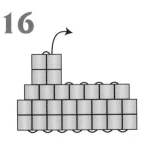

Stitch back through these first two sets of beads to stabilize them.
(Illustrations 15 & 16)